I0816436

JOURNAL OF THE
PSYCHONAUT

MULTIDISCIPLINARY ASSOCIATION FOR PSYCHEDELIC STUDIES

This journal is intended for personal use pertaining to wellness and health. No authors or collaborators on this journal are advising psychedelic use. This journal is not intended to treat or prescribe the user. The user of this journal understands psychedelic use is illegal.

Co-published by Synergetic Press and the Multidisciplinary Association for Psychedelic Studies (MAPS).

Synergetic Press | 1 Bluebird Court, Santa Fe, NM 87508
& 24 Old Gloucester St. London, WC1N 3AL England

Multidisciplinary Association for Psychedelic Studies (MAPS)
PO Box 8423, Santa Cruz, CA 95061

ISBN 9798985012231

Cover design by Ryan Beauregard
Interior design by Jonathan Hahn
Content Creators and Strategists: Jenny Neal, Grace Cepe
Managing Editor: Amanda Müller
Developmental Editor: Noelle Armstrong
Production Editor: Allison Felus

Printed in Thailand

WELCOME, PSYCHONAUT!

This is an invitation to explore your inner universe.

Psychedelic experiences have the potential to dramatically change us for the better, but only if we truly integrate what we've learned from them into our everyday lives. This journal is your sacred space to prepare for and then integrate these lessons from your explorations of nonordinary states of consciousness.

We encourage you to color outside the lines, break the rules, and above all else work with this journal in the way that fits *you* best.

SET THE SETTING

Psychedelic experiences can vary tremendously and are sometimes unpredictable, but in general they are most influenced by your mindset, your setting, and of course the drug itself.

"Set the setting" is a principle that invites you to approach your journey with clear intention, a resolve to face your shadow, and a commitment to ongoing integration.

> "MDMA-assisted psychotherapy is inner-directed, meaning the therapeutic content and the direction of the session is informed primarily by the participant and their inner healing intelligence. The participant's relationship with their internal source of power will outlast the course of treatment and their relationship with the therapists. When a participant is (re) acquainted with the confidence that they can lead a healthful life, they get to reap the rewards of their hard work and know it was them who made it happen. In the same way, at some point a well-cared-for plant will outgrow its greenhouse shelter, and go out into the world with the health and strength to protect itself and sustain its own life."
>
> —Shannon Clare Carlin, MA

BEFORE

Proper preparation for any experience of nonordinary states of consciousness—psychedelically induced or not–can greatly impact the way your journey unfolds.

Consider these questions before you embark on your exploration:

- Do I feel safe?
- Have I taken proper harm-reduction precautions before my journey?
- What is my intention for embarking on this journey?
- What hesitations or reservations am I carrying with me, and what can I do to let them go?
- How do I feel in my body?
- Are my surroundings set up in a way that feels nourishing to me?
- Do I have trusted friends and loved ones to reach out to for support?

If needed, The Fireside Project is a psychedelic peer-support hotline that can provide emotional assistance both during and after psychedelic experiences. Call 62-FIRESIDE.

> "Early media on the use of psychedelics to treat trauma has focused primarily on combat veterans, a vast majority of whom are men. Without careful attention paid to make psychedelic therapy safe and inviting for BIPOC folx, women, and people who are genderqueer or transgender, norms which make it safer for people of privilege - but not everyone - to participate in such healing will only intensify."
>
> —**Betty Aldworth, MAPS' Director of Communications**

DURING

Allow the experience to unfold.

Challenging experiences, emotions, and memories may come to the surface. If they do, remember this Zendo Project principle: *Difficult is not bad.*

> "I hope in the big picture, by 2050, we'll have enough people with an understanding of how to use psychedelics for personal, emotional, and spiritual growth that we'll have a more spiritualized humanity to turn us more towards saving the planet from mass weapons, climate change, and prejudice"
>
> —**Rick Doblin, PhD**

AFTER

Self-care is important every day, but it's especially important after a psychedelic experience.

Consider asking yourselves these questions during the aftercare period of the integration process:

- Am I well rested, fed, and hydrated?
- What key insights, messages, or "aha" moments occurred for me?
- What emotions came up during my experience?
- What sensations did I feel in my body?
- What parts of myself did I meet again? What parts of myself, if any, did I let go of?
- How do I want to integrate this experience in my everyday life?

THE 7 PRINCIPLES OF MAPS

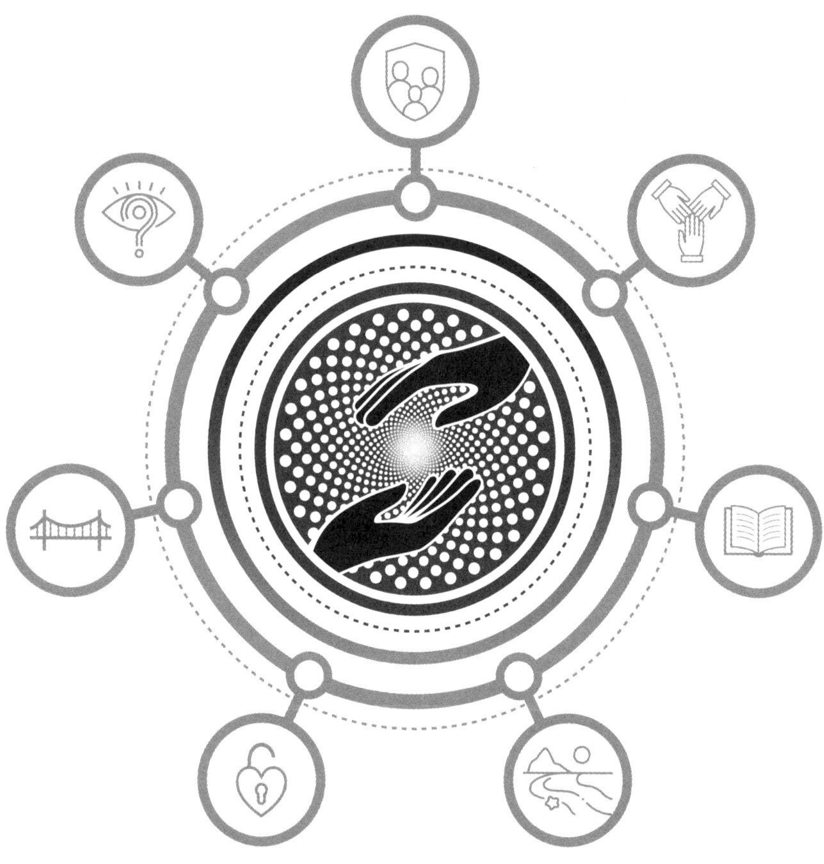

HEALING FOR ALL

We proactively and creatively work to overcome cultural, legal, and economic barriers to equitable psychedelic access. We work to catalyze mass mental health and spirituality with the belief that saving one life saves a whole world.

PRIORITIZE PUBLIC BENEFIT

We prioritize the good of our collective humanity and planet over organizational or individual gain. We strive to honor the communities, ancestral and modern traditions, and struggles we have learned from by practicing reciprocity and working for the good of future generations.

OPEN SCIENCE, OPEN BOOKS

We commit to sharing what we learn and create, including our findings, protocols, and finances. Transparency creates a culture of accountability and contributes to the public domain, facilitating ethical collaboration toward a greater shared purpose.

SET THE SETTING

We approach everything we do like a journey: with clear intention, a resolve to face our shadow, and a commitment to ongoing integration. Guided by history and inspired by visionary possibilities, we aim to build foundations and tools for symbiotic and inclusive ecosystems.

CONSCIOUSNESS WITHOUT CRIMINALIZATION

We advocate for the dignity and rights of all people who use drugs, free from fear and stigma. We firmly reject criminalization of people growing, making, distributing, or using drugs.

BE THE BRIDGE

We build common ground between the medical, the mystical, the marginalized, and the mainstream. Uniting divergent communities and traversing new territory demands spiritual audacity.

SEE PAST THE PARADOX

We take an incremental approach to radical change. We employ a diversity of tactics, perspectives, and strategies because we recognize the wisdom that unites seemingly paradoxical approaches. Everyone carries a piece of the puzzle.